~~~~~~

THE MISSION OF THE SUPER BIG SISTER/BROTHER ADVENTURES BRAND IS TO GIVE EACH AND EVERY CHILD ACKNOWLEDGMENT AND PRIDE IN THEIR NEW ROLE AS A BIG SISTER OR BIG BROTHER. OUR PRODUCTS SEEK TO NOT ONLY WELCOME THE NEW ADDITION TO YOUR FAMILY BUT TO CELEBRATE AND ENCOURAGE THE NEW ROLE, JOY, AND MEMORIES THAT EACH IN EVERY CHILD WILL EXPERIENCE AS A SUPER BIG SISTER OR AS A SUPER BIG BROTHER.

~~~~~~

COPYRIGHT © 2019 BY SUPERBIG SB ADVENTURES
ALL RIGHTS RESERVED. THIS BOOK OR ANY PORTION THEREOF MAY NOT BE REPRODUCED OR USED IN ANY MANNER WHATSOEVER WITHOUT THE EXPRESS WRITTEN PERMISSION OF THE PUBLISHER EXCEPT FOR THE USE OF BRIEF QUOTATIONS IN A BOOK REVIEW.

PRINTED IN THE UNITED STATES OF AMERICA

ISBN: 978-1-7336128-2-1

SUPERBIG SISTER/BROTHER ADVENTURES
WWW.SUPERBIGSB.COM

Braylen,
Keep Flying!
Keep Soaring!
LS

DEDICATED...

TO MY HEARTBEATS, MY FAMILY, MY REASON.
THANK YOU FOR LISTENING TO MY DREAMS
& CELEBRATING MY JOYS.
ETERNAL LOVE,
~ LUCY

TO MY DAUGHTER SLOAN WHO IS THE
BRIGHT LIGHT OF MY EVERYDAY AND A
BEAUTIFUL SUPER BIG SISTER.
WITH LOVE,
~ JOLENNA

TO MY FAMILY WHO IS THE BIGGEST SUPPORT
SYSTEM AND REASON TO LOVE.
LOVE,
~ DISHA

Deja, now you are a SUPER BIG SISTER!

SWOOSH!!!!

AND SO,
BEGINS THE ADVENTURES OF DEJA,
SUPER BIG SISTER!

TO BE CONTINUED...

READ MORE ADVENTURES...
AS OUR HERO CONTINUES TO HELP:

"HEY BABY" (AT THE HOSPITAL)

"HOUSE HAVOC" (AT HOME)

"A GRAND TIME" (AT GRANDPARENTS HOUSE)

"SWINGS, SAND, SHENANIGANS!" (AT THE PARK)

"BOOK BREAK" (AT THE LIBRARY)

"POUTS & POKES" (AT THE DOCTOR'S OFFICE)

"CEREAL AVALANCHE" (AT THE GROCERY STORE)

"WAVY WEEKEND" (AT THE BEACH)

STORIES AND ILLUSTRATIONS BY
LUCY SAMS AND JOLENNA MAPES

DON'T FORGET TO ORDER YOUR VERY OWN SUPER BIG T-SHIRT AT:
www.superbigsb.com

Made in the USA
Columbia, SC
06 June 2019